Original title:
Silent Goodbye

Copyright © 2024 Swan Charm
All rights reserved.

Author: Sebastian Sarapuu
ISBN HARDBACK: 978-9916-79-158-5
ISBN PAPERBACK: 978-9916-79-159-2
ISBN EBOOK: 978-9916-79-160-8

A Seraph's Sigh

In twilight's glow, a gentle breath,
A whisper soft, beyond mere death.
Angels weep for bonds once grand,
Their wings outstretched, in love they stand.

With every tear, a story told,
Of faith unyielding, hearts of gold.
In silence wrapped, sweet memories bind,
A solace found, in grace entwined.

The heavens hum a sacred song,
Where prayers linger, where we belong.
Each note a promise, softly flows,
In quietude, the spirit knows.

And as we part, our souls ignites,
In twilight's arms, where day invites.
A path of light, where love will guide,
Through veils of tears, where hope resides.

For even when we say goodbye,
The heart will speak, the soul will fly.
In faith's embrace, our lives shall blend,
A silent tide, that knows no end.

Sacred Shadows of Absence

In the stillness of the night,
Whispers of the lost take flight.
In shadows deep, their essence glows,
Reminders of the love we chose.

Each tear we shed, a silent prayer,
To the heavens, our thoughts laid bare.
In absence felt, their spirits soar,
In memories held, forevermore.

Celestial Adieu

Stars blink softly in the night,
A farewell wrapped in gentle light.
As they ascend beyond our gaze,
We honor them in twilight's haze.

With every dawn, their presence flows,
A sacred bond that never goes.
In every breath, a heartbeat's trace,
A celestial love, an endless grace.

Tranquil Departure

The river flows with whispers clear,
Of those who loved, now ever near.
In tranquil moments, peace we find,
With every thought, they're intertwined.

The sun dips low, the day must fold,
Yet in our hearts, their stories told.
In aching hearts, a soothing balm,
In every memory, a sacred calm.

The Lament of Lost Souls

In the shadows, voices wail,
Of dreams once bright, now frail.
Each spirit wanders, seeking peace,
In endless night, their cries won't cease.

With every sigh, we weigh the cost,
Of love remembered, of moments lost.
In prayers we lift, their souls take flight,
In the embrace of eternal light.

Soft Footsteps Among the Stars

In the quiet night, we tread so light,
Each whisper of faith, guides our flight.
Beneath the heavens, where dreams align,
Soft footsteps dance, in love divine.

The moon looks down with a knowing smile,
As we walk in grace, through every trial.
Stars twinkle bright, our path they trace,
In celestial halls, we find our place.

The Celestial Call of Departure

A trumpet sounds, from heavens afar,
Echoing softly, like a guiding star.
With hearts ablaze, we rise and soar,
To the call of love, forevermore.

In the twilight glow, our spirits ascend,
Each bond we cherish, yet must defend.
Through valleys of time, we journey wide,
Following whispers of the holy guide.

A Labyrinth of Unspoken Goodbyes

In shadows deep, where sorrows blend,
The heart knows paths, it cannot mend.
Words unsaid linger, like fading light,
In the labyrinth of love, we face the night.

Each face we meet, a fleeting grace,
A reminder that time cannot erase.
In silent tears, we grasp what's gone,
But hope remains, through the dawn's bright song.

The Melodic Silence of Parting

As the day fades, whispers fill the air,
In melodic silence, we lay our prayer.
With every breath, hearts intertwined,
In the depth of quiet, peace we find.

Every footfall soft, like gentle rain,
Gathering memories, joy and pain.
In stillness, we learn of love's embrace,
The beauty found, in the sacred space.

Shadows of a Holy Departure

In shadows cast by love's great grace,
We gather round this sacred space.
As whispers lift to heavens high,
We bow our heads, and softly cry.

A journey starts, a soul takes flight,
Embraced by warmth, dispelling night.
With every tear, a prayer we weave,
In faith, we stand and still believe.

The light of dawn breaks through the dark,
Each heartbeat echoes heaven's spark.
A final breath, a life set free,
In love's embrace, eternity.

So raise our voices, let them soar,
In honor of the life before.
For in the shadows, love remains,
A holy bond that never wanes.

The Quiet Benediction

A moment still, a breath so sweet,
Within this space, our hearts shall meet.
The silence sings a hallowed tune,
Beneath the watchful, gentle moon.

We seek the peace of sacred vows,
To honor love; we humbly bow.
In every sigh and whispered prayer,
Divine connection lingers there.

With tender grace, we share the light,
Anointing souls, dispelling night.
Each blessing cast, a fragrant rose,
In quietude, true beauty grows.

So let our spirits gently rise,
In the soft glow of starlit skies.
A benediction, pure and clear,
May love hold fast, forever near.

Glimmers of Eternal Light

Upon the path of life we tread,
With glimmers bright, the light we spread.
In every heart, a spark ignites,
Illuminating darkest nights.

Through trials faced and burdens borne,
When hope seems lost, we are reborn.
The radiance within our soul,
A guiding star, it makes us whole.

United in this holy grace,
We chase the shadows, find our place.
In every smile, a glimpse we see,
The love that binds you close to me.

So let us walk this sacred way,
In glimmers bright, our spirits sway.
For in this journey's ebb and flow,
Eternal light will ever glow.

A Pause Before the Heavens

In silent pause, we take a breath,
Before the door of life and death.
The weight of time, a heavy shroud,
In reverence, we stand, unbowed.

With eyes uplifted to the skies,
We seek the truth beneath the lies.
In quiet moments, wisdom stirs,
Between the lines of sacred words.

With open hearts, we share our fears,
In voices soft, we shed our tears.
Yet hope remains, a candle's glow,
In every heart, love's currents flow.

As breaths align with stillness deep,
We honor souls that gently leap.
A pause before the heavens wide,
In faith, we trust, they'll be our guide.

A Celestial Transition

In the silence, stars align,
Whispers of the divine,
Heaven's door swings wide,
Guiding souls to abide.

Mighty hands reach above,
Embraced by light and love,
Journey onward we must,
In faith, in hope, in trust.

The moonlight dances slow,
Casting shadows below,
In this sacred space,
We find our rightful place.

From earth we writhe and spin,
To the song without sin,
Souls ascend to the sky,
In peace the spirits fly.

A vision pure and bright,
Wrapped in endless night,
Each heartbeat is a prayer,
Transcending all despair.

In the Embrace of Meaning

In the stillness of the morn,
New blessings are reborn,
With each breath, we aspire,
To nourish love's sweet fire.

Each heartbeat sings a tune,
Under the watchful moon,
Waves of grace, a tide,
Where our spirits coincide.

Through valleys deep and wide,
In faith we will abide,
Every moment we see,
A glimpse of eternity.

In the arms of tender truth,
We cherish eternal youth,
With wisdom as our guide,
In meaning, we reside.

Together, hand in hand,
On sacred, timeless land,
We seek, we find, we grow,
In love's embrace, we flow.

The Unvoiced Lord's Call

In the quiet of the night,
Voices soft, pure light,
The Lord's call, so gentle,
Through shadows, it's essential.

Awake, souls of the lost,
Know the Savior's cost,
In silence, find your way,
To the dawn of every day.

Hearts open to the cries,
As the morning sun tries,
Breaking chains that confine,
In grace, our spirits shine.

The unspoken truth of time,
Is our lives in their prime,
Surrender to the call,
In faith, we rise, not fall.

In the dance of fate and will,
Trust the sacred thrill,
For each step is a prayer,
In the Lord's love, we care.

Graceful Farewell to the Earthbound

As daylight fades away,
We prepare to sway,
From the worldly embrace,
To a higher place.

With gratitude, we yield,
In this open field,
Souls intertwined in grace,
Leaving a sacred space.

The journey has been long,
To the notes of a song,
With each step we have tread,
Remembering the dead.

A farewell to the ties,
As the spirit flies,
In the hands of the One,
Our new journey begun.

Embrace the light ahead,
Let go of all dread,
In faith, we trust the flight,
To celestial realms of light.

The Embrace of the Unseen

In the stillness of the night,
Whispers drift on sacred air.
Hearts entwined in faith's embrace,
Guided by love's unyielding care.

Veils of silence, truths revealed,
In shadows cast by holy light.
Souls connected, spirit healed,
A glimpse of grace in the quiet fight.

In dreams we walk, hand in hand,
Where hope blooms like spring's first flower.
Faith, an anchor, love a strand,
Uniting us in every hour.

Though eyes may close, we still see,
The bonds that death cannot sever.
In the embrace of the unseen,
We find peace, now and forever.

Twilight Blessings of Departure

As daylight fades and twilight glows,
We gather close in sacred trust.
With whispered prayers and gentle prose,
We honor love, so deep and just.

Each tear reflects a story dear,
Memories woven in golden threads.
With every sigh, we draw them near,
In the twilight, where silence spreads.

Through parting paths, we find our way,
In stars that shine through darkest night.
A blessing shared as shadows sway,
Guided by faith's unwavering light.

Feel the warmth of grace surround,
In every heartbeat, love shall dwell.
In whispered goodbyes, hope is found,
Twilight blessings cast their spell.

Breaking Bread in Memory's Light

Around the table, hands are joined,
A sacred meal with love is shared.
In each crumb, a heart is coined,
In every sip, a soul is bared.

Stories echo, laughter flows,
In this moment, time stands still.
With gratitude, our spirit grows,
In memory's light, we drink our fill.

The taste of life, both sweet and bitter,
Each morsel holds a mystic bond.
Through every bite, our spirits glitter,
In unity, our hearts respond.

As bread is broken, so are ties,
In the shared light, we are renewed.
Connected souls, never demise,
In love's embrace, we are imbued.

The Angel's Quiet Farewell

In the hush of twilight's grace,
An angel whispers soft and low.
With gentle wings, a loving trace,
A farewell wrapped in sacred glow.

Eyes closed in peace, hearts weep in light,
As journeys end in realms above.
With every breath, a soul takes flight,
Guided home through endless love.

Timeless echoes, prayers rise,
Through clouds of hope, their spirit sings.
With each goodbye, a new sunrise,
In love's embrace, all heartache brings.

Though parting brings a heavy sigh,
In the silence, comfort stays.
The angel's watch, a lullaby,
In quiet farewell, love displays.

Transcendence in Stillness

In the silence of the morn,
I seek the sacred light.
Whispers of the universe,
Guide me through the night.

In the stillness, hearts converge,
Threads of grace entwine.
Every breath a prayer,
In this moment divine.

Time dissolves in twilight's glow,
Peace settles like a dove.
In this calm, I find my truth,
Wrapped in boundless love.

Beyond the veil of earthly cares,
I reach for what is known.
Transcending all my fears,
To a heart that feels like home.

As the stars begin to fade,
I hold the stillness tight.
In the quiet, I am whole,
Bathed in endless light.

A Last Prayer in the Night

In shadowed corners of the soul,
I whisper soft and low.
A final prayer before the dawn,
To the heavens, I bestow.

Each word a note upon the breeze,
Carried far and wide.
In faith, I find my anchor,
In grace, my gentle guide.

The stars bear witness to my plea,
A flicker in the dark.
With every heartbeat, I relent,
Igniting sacred spark.

Through pain and trials, I have walked,
Yet here, I find release.
In every sigh, redemption's song,
Embracing perfect peace.

As night enfolds the weary world,
My spirit takes its flight.
In unity with all that is,
A last prayer in the night.

Ephemeral Embrace

In fleeting moments, love arrives,
A soft and tender touch.
Like petals whispering to the wind,
Reminders mean so much.

Time dances lightly on the soul,
A spark that brightly glows.
In every heartbeat, I can feel,
The essence of what flows.

With every breath, a legacy,
Each sigh a timeless grace.
In the ephemeral embrace,
I find my sacred place.

The beauty lies in letting go,
In trusting the unseen.
For in the grasp of fleeting time,
Eternity is gleaned.

So I hold these moments dear,
With gratitude, I rise.
In the dance of life, I find,
A love that never dies.

The Quiet Ascension

In stillness, there's a rising flame,
A gentle lifting tide.
Awakening the soul within,
Embracing spirit's glide.

With each step upon this path,
I listen to the call.
The quiet ascension of my heart,
Is answering it all.

Mountains may loom high above,
Yet faith will be my guide.
Through valleys deep, I wander forth,
With peace ever inside.

In every challenge, a lesson waits,
In every tear, a sign.
The quiet ascension lifts my voice,
As souls in union shine.

So let me soar on wings of grace,
Into the endless light.
In the quiet ascension, I transcend,
Embracing sacred sight.

The Ascending Heart

In the stillness of the morning light,
The heart begins to sing its praise,
Lifting spirits toward the height,
Guided by love's gentle ways.

Each prayer a whisper in the breeze,
A call to grace, a sacred sound,
In quiet moments, faith will seize,
And in this peace, our souls are found.

As dawn breaks forth, the shadows flee,
The radiant warmth does share its part,
With every breath, we come to see,
The beauty of the ascending heart.

Through trials faced and burdens borne,
Our hopes, they soar like birds in flight,
From darkness, into light reborn,
Embracing all that feels so right.

So let us rise, united, strong,
In faith, our hearts will never part,
Together singing love's sweet song,
Forever held by the ascending heart.

When Souls Take Flight

Upon the wings of love we rise,
Beyond the bounds of earthly chains,
In faith, we reach beyond the skies,
And feel the joy that freedom gains.

When sorrow fades and hope ignites,
Our essence soars to realms unknown,
In sacred dance, our spirit lights,
As angels guide us gently home.

With every heartbeat, truth unfolds,
In whispers shared, our hearts unite,
In love's embrace, through silence bold,
Together, we shall take our flight.

For souls entwined in grace will find,
The beauty of a higher call,
As heaven's love, in ties entwined,
Awakens us, we shall not fall.

So let us soar with vibrant might,
Through realms of peace, our spirits bright,
In holy harmony, we rise,
When souls take flight, our hearts the prize.

Beneath the Cloak of Solitude

In silence, wisdom softly speaks,
A gentle echo through the night,
With shadows cast on weary peaks,
We seek the path, we feel the light.

In solitude, our hearts refine,
A sacred space where dreams are sown,
Amidst the stars, where hopes align,
We find the love that feels like home.

The whispers of the night unfold,
A tapestry of stars up high,
In every breath, we come to hold,
The beauty of this quiet sky.

Beneath the cloak, the spirit breathes,
In tender moments, fears dissolve,
In darkness may our light bequeath,
The strength to rise, to heal, evolve.

So let us walk the path alone,
In solitude, our hearts will greet,
The sacred truth within our own,
Beneath the cloak, our souls complete.

Hushed Hymns at Dusk

As daylight wanes, the shadows blend,
The world around begins to sigh,
In whispered prayers, we find our mend,
And raise our voices 'neath the sky.

Hushed hymns arise, a reverent call,
In unity, our spirits soar,
In twilight's glow, we choose to fall,
Into the arms of love's great shore.

With every note, our hearts aligned,
We weave a tapestry of grace,
In dusky moments, truth defined,
Embracing every sacred space.

The evening star, a guide above,
Illuminates our fervent trust,
In silence, we can always love,
As hearts unite, and fears combust.

So let us sing as dusk descends,
In softly woven melodies,
In hushed hymns, where peace transcends,
At sunset's glow, our spirits ease.

Veils of Faith and Farewell

In shadows deep, our spirits soar,
With whispered prayers, we seek the shore.
Veils of faith, drawn close in trust,
Embracing love, in hearts we must.

As echoes fade, the light grows bright,
In every tear, a spark ignites.
Farewell is but a step, a sign,
In sacred bonds, our souls align.

Through trials faced, our hearts will mend,
In unity, we find our blend.
With veils of faith, we walk the path,
And greet the dawn, escaping wrath.

As journey's end draws ever near,
In every heart, there's faith to steer.
We rise again, in hope's embrace,
To find our peace, in endless grace.

In whispered winds, the truth resounds,
In every prayer, our love abounds.
Veils of faith, though thin and frail,
Guide us through each heartfelt trail.

The Gift of Silence

In moments lost, the silence speaks,
A gentle balm for restless weeks.
In quietude, our souls align,
The gift of peace, a sacred sign.

Beneath the stars, where whispers dwell,
The heart learns secrets, stories to tell.
In stillness found, we hear the call,
To give our all, to rise, not fall.

From chaos born, the silence springs,
In gentle folds, the spirit sings.
In every pause, divinity's grace,
A tender touch, in time and space.

As shadows dance in evening's breath,
The gift of silence conquers death.
In silent prayer, we find our way,
Illuminated by dawn's soft ray.

Hold fast to grace, let silence lead,
In every heart, there lies a seed.
The gift of silence, pure and bright,
Transforms our souls, ignites our light.

In the Garden of Grace

In the garden, where blossoms bloom,
Silent whispers erase the gloom.
With faith as roots, and love as seed,
In grace we find, all hearts are freed.

The sun bestows its golden rays,
Guiding seekers through life's maze.
In every petal, beauty grows,
In stillness, divine love flows.

Through trials faced, and storms that rage,
We seek the wisdom of each page.
In the garden, our souls entwine,
In sacred soil, the heart's design.

With every prayer, the flowers rise,
Painting hope beneath the skies.
In the garden, we long to rest,
Embraced by love, forever blessed.

In twilight's glow, a promise made,
In the garden, no fears invade.
With grace abounding, peace shall reign,
In hearts united, joy remains.

Angelic Shadows at Dusk

As day retreats and night unfolds,
Angelic shadows whisper gold.
In twilight's hush, the spirit wakes,
To see the light that love partakes.

With gentle wings, they guide our way,
In every heart, their truths convey.
Beneath the stars that softly gleam,
We find our strength in every dream.

In silence deep, their voices call,
Reminding us we're never small.
In every struggle, every strife,
Angelic grace supports our life.

Through darkened paths, they light the scene,
In every moment, love is seen.
Trust in the shadows, hold them tight,
For in their care, we'll find our light.

With faith renewed, as night descends,
In angelic shadows, love transcends.
At dusk we soar, our spirits free,
In sacred love, eternally.

Soulful Surrender in Reverence

In the stillness, hearts unite,
Offering praise, seeking light.
Hands uplifted, spirits soar,
In humble silence, we adore.

Minds in prayer, eyes closed tight,
Whispers echo through the night.
Faith like rivers, ever wide,
In this moment, we abide.

Voices blend, a sacred hymn,
In His grace, we find our kin.
Every heartbeat, echoes true,
In surrender, we renew.

Sharing burdens, lifting souls,
Together we seek our goals.
In every tear, a story told,
In gentle warmth, love unfolds.

With every step, His path we trace,
Guided softly by His grace.
In reverence, we walk this day,
Surrendered to His way.

Dreams of a Shared Tomorrow

In unity, our dreams take flight,
Hand in hand, we seek the light.
Voices merging, songs divine,
In harmony, our hearts entwine.

Hope is whispered in the breeze,
A promise held, our spirits seize.
Through trials faced, together we stand,
Trusting in the One who planned.

Fields of gold and skies so blue,
In every vision, love breaks through.
Together we can build anew,
A future bright, for me and you.

Each step forward, guided, sure,
In shared dreams, we find the cure.
Through open hearts, let kindness flow,
In a shared tomorrow, hope will grow.

The Light Beyond the Veil

In shadows deep, the light will break,
A gentle whisper, hope awake.
Beyond the veil, a sight so bright,
Guiding souls through darkest night.

Promises woven in the stars,
Healing wounds, mending scars.
With every breath, we draw so near,
In His presence, cast out fear.

Morning rises, darkness fades,
In His love, our path is laid.
In every trial, strength bestowed,
His mercy flows, our hearts erode.

Timeless grace, forever real,
In quiet moments, we can feel.
The light beyond, forever stays,
Guiding each step in His ways.

A Faint Whisper in the Wind

In whispers soft, the Spirit calls,
Through rustling leaves, His message falls.
In every breeze, His love unfolds,
In tender tales, His truth is told.

Listening close, we find our peace,
In every sigh, our worries cease.
A dance of leaves, a song of grace,
In nature's arms, we find our place.

The world may roar, yet still we stand,
Embracing hope, hand in hand.
In softest moments, hearts align,
With every heartbeat, His love shines.

A gentle nudge, a guiding star,
In silent prayer, we wander far.
With every breath, the spirit flows,
A faint whisper, forever knows.

The Veil of Sacred Absence

In silence deep, the heart does pine,
A whisper soft, of truth divine.
The veil descends, on tender grace,
A sacred space, where shadows trace.

In longing's grip, the soul takes flight,
Through realms of dark, toward holy light.
The absence swells, yet hope remains,
In every tear, love's gentle strains.

The echoes fade, yet still they sing,
Of promises made, and the joy they bring.
In quietude, we feel the call,
To rise again, though fractured, fall.

With every breath, our faith is stretched,
In sacred voids, our hearts are etched.
The veil may hide, but can't obscure,
The love that flows, steadfast and pure.

Through all the storms, the calm persists,
In woven threads, we find the bliss.
The sacred absence teaches well,
In empty space, our spirits dwell.

In the Stillness of the Spirit

In quiet dawn, the spirit wakes,
A gentle breeze, the silence breaks.
Amongst the still, the heart will hear,
The sacred truth, forever near.

Each breath a prayer, pure and sweet,
In stillness found, our souls will meet.
The light of grace, it softly glows,
Within the depths, where wisdom flows.

In a moment's pause, the world refrains,
The steady pulse of love remains.
The inner voice, it guides us through,
In every thought, the light breaks through.

With open hearts, we seek His face,
In calm repose, we feel His grace.
The stillness speaks, a sacred art,
As love unfolds within the heart.

In every shadow, hope will rise,
In quietude, we hear the cries.
The spirit whispers, soft and low,
In stillness found, our hearts will glow.

The Gentle Unraveling

In time's embrace, the threads unwind,
A tapestry, divinely lined.
Each gentle pull reveals a tale,
Of love and loss, of hope not frail.

The heart expands, through pain and joy,
In every seam, the soul's employ.
Each layer shed, a life made clear,
In unraveling, we draw near.

A cosmic dance, of ebb and flow,
With every twist, new paths we sow.
In tender light, the shadows blend,
As love's foundation will not end.

In every tear, a grace bestowed,
The gentle unraveling, a road.
Through all that breaks, we find the whole,
In every fissure, the perfect soul.

Thus let us weave, with open hearts,
A fabric bright, where love imparts.
Through gentle hands, the journey's made,
In unraveling, our fears allayed.

A Covenant of Love Unspoken

In whispered vows, our spirits bind,
A sacred trust, in silence signed.
Beyond the words, the heart may speak,
In every glance, the strong and meek.

Through trials faced, together strong,
In faith we find, where we belong.
A bond unformed, yet deeply felt,
In every moment, love is dealt.

With open arms, we shelter grace,
In every smile, we find our place.
The covenant blooms, a flower bright,
In unison, we share the light.

In gentle gestures, love's revealed,
A promise made, a heart congealed.
Though words may fade, our truth remains,
In silent rhythms, love sustains.

So let us tread this path with care,
In joy and sorrow, we will share.
A covenant forged, in time's embrace,
A love unspoken, endless grace.

Wings of Faith on an Unknown Journey

When shadows lengthen on the ground,
We rise on wings, through lost and found.
A path unseen, where hearts must tread,
In faith we walk, though fears are fed.

With every step, the spirit glows,
Guided by light that softly flows.
Love leads us forth to realms unknown,
In trust we wander, never alone.

The stars above serenely guide,
Through valleys deep and rivers wide.
Each moment blessed, a sacred thread,
Of hope and grace as we are led.

Through trials fierce and gentle grace,
We find strength in this sacred space.
Where whispers of truth softly call,
We shall not falter, we shall not fall.

In every heart, a flame does rise,
Illuminating the darkest skies.
With wings of faith, our spirits soar,
Embracing love forevermore.

The Echo of Pious Goodbyes

In quiet moments, voices blend,
Pious hearts with love to send.
Each parting kiss, a tender sigh,
As souls take flight, we wave goodbye.

In hallowed halls where prayers reside,
The echoes linger, none to hide.
A tapestry of moments shared,
In sacred bonds, we are prepared.

With every tear and smile combined,
The bonds of faith forever bind.
Though distance grows, the spirit stays,
Embracing love in countless ways.

As shadows fall and lights grow dim,
We find our strength in hymns within.
God's gentle hand, our guiding light,
Illuminates our darkest night.

And as the sun begins to set,
We gather hopes, no room for regret.
In every heart, a promise lies,
The strength of faith, no need for goodbyes.

The Heart's Whisper of Departure

A quiet breath, a whispered plea,
As time unfolds, we yearn to be.
In moments still, the heart takes flight,
To lands unknown, beyond our sight.

The gentle call of distant shores,
Awakens dreams, our spirit soars.
With each farewell, a chapter closed,
Yet love remains, forever prose.

In prayers offered, we find our peace,
With every step, our doubts release.
The heart's soft voice, a guiding star,
In light and love, we travel far.

The bonds we forged, the hands we held,
In sacred trust, our souls compelled.
Though paths may part, we stand as one,
In faith united, we have begun.

As we depart, and journeys start,
Each whispered hope, an open heart.
With grace bestowed, we'll find our way,
In love eternal, night or day.

A Shroud of Celestial Quiet

In stillness deep, where shadows play,
A hush descends, the end of day.
The heavens echo soft and bright,
In a shroud of peace, we find our light.

The stars above, like candles glow,
Illuminating paths below.
In silence wrapped, our spirits soar,
To realms of calm, forevermore.

With every breath, a prayer is sent,
In reverent calm, our souls relent.
The quiet calls, a gentle guide,
Where faith and love forever bide.

Each moment still, a sacred thread,
In love's embrace, our hearts are fed.
Through trials faced, we stand as one,
With grateful hearts, the battle won.

As twilight wanes and night draws near,
The whispers soothe, dispelling fear.
In celestial quiet, we shall rest,
Embracing peace, forever blessed.

In the Stillness, He Remains

In the quiet dawn of grace,
Whispers of His love embrace.
He walks beside the weary soul,
In the stillness, we're made whole.

Mountains bow and oceans part,
In the silence, He imparts.
A gentle hand upon our hearts,
His light in darkness, never departs.

Through the shadows, faith does rise,
In storms, a calm that never lies.
Trust leads us through the night,
In the stillness, He is light.

Every tear that falls in prayer,
Echoes of our burdens bare.
He listens to each longing sigh,
In the stillness, He is nigh.

From the depths to heights we climb,
In His timing, all is divine.
Rest assured, He holds the reins,
In the stillness, He remains.

The Reflection of Eternal Bonds

In the mirror of the soul,
Love reflects, it makes us whole.
Through trials faced and joys embraced,
Eternal bonds cannot be replaced.

Hand in hand, we walk this way,
Guided by light, come what may.
In every smile, in every tear,
The presence of Him, ever near.

Fleeting moments, yet timeless grace,
In every heartbeat, we find our place.
His promise woven through our days,
In the reflection, love's embrace.

Across the expanse of shifting time,
Every cry, each prayer, a rhyme.
In our hearts, His truth resounds,
The reflection of eternal bounds.

As the stars illuminate the night,
So do our souls in sacred light.
With faith as our unyielding sword,
In His love, we are restored.

Beneath the Watchful Skies

Beneath the watchful skies above,
We seek the peace of holy love.
Stars align, a map divine,
In every heartbeat, a sacred sign.

Clouds may gather, storms may roar,
Yet in our hearts, He is the shore.
In every trial, we find our way,
Beneath the skies, we learn to pray.

Nature sings a hymn so sweet,
In every breeze, His grace we meet.
Mountains rise as temples stand,
Beneath watchful skies, we are His hand.

The moonlight whispers tales of old,
Guiding us with visions bold.
In silence deep, the truth unfurls,
Beneath the skies, a love that swirls.

So let us walk with hearts aligned,
In faith, our spirits intertwined.
Underneath the heavens' dome,
Beneath the watchful skies, we roam.

Remembrance in the Sacred Void

In sacred void, where silence speaks,
The heart finds strength that never flees.
In stillness deep, our souls ignite,
Remembrance cloaked in holy light.

Every echo, a whisper of grace,
In the shadows, we find His face.
Where hope may flicker, faith will grow,
In remembrance, love will show.

Through trials faced, we gather here,
In the sacred void, without fear.
Each step a testament of trust,
In remembrance, rise we must.

Hands uplifted, hearts in prayer,
In the stillness, we lay bare.
Through the void, His presence calls,
In remembrance, love enthralls.

So let us dwell in this embrace,
Finding solace in His grace.
In every heartbeat, we rejoice,
Remembrance in our sacred voice.

Lullabies of Solace and Peace

In quiet night, the stars do gleam,
God's gentle hands, they guide our dream.
Each whisper soft, a healing balm,
Bringing the heart a perfect calm.

With every breath, let worries cease,
In faith we find our sweet release.
A melody of grace divine,
In stillness, love's bright light will shine.

For in the shadows, hope will rise,
Wrapped in the warmth of endless skies.
We cherish moments, pure and bright,
Lullabies' gift in the quiet night.

Embrace the dawn, let peace unfold,
His promises, in whispers bold.
In every heart, His presence gleams,
A sacred light that softly beams.

So close your eyes and drift away,
Into the arms where angels play.
In deep repose, find solace true,
For every prayer brings peace anew.

The Gentle Tides of Time

The waves they come and softly go,
In rhythmic dance, we find the flow.
Each moment cherished, time does weave,
A tapestry of grace, believe.

As sunsets fade, the stars align,
The universe sings, and love is divine.
Through seasons' change, His hand we trace,
In every sorrow, we find His grace.

The moonlight bathes our weary souls,
In silent nights, His voice consoles.
With every tide, our spirits lift,
In gentle ebb, we find our gift.

So let us walk where waters meet,
In sacred paths, He guides our feet.
With every step, the heart will see,
The gentle tides that set us free.

In trust we stand, for time is kind,
A promise held in heart and mind.
Together we shall brave the storm,
In sacred love, our souls are warm.

A Glimpse of Infinite Love

In every heart, His love abides,
A sacred truth through countless tides.
In every moment, grace unfolds,
A glimpse of warmth, a love that holds.

Upon the winds, His kindness flows,
Through every trial, His mercy grows.
A gentle touch in every prayer,
Infinite love beyond compare.

The sun will rise, His light will shine,
Illuminating souls divine.
In humble hearts, His joy is found,
In every lost, another's sound.

So lift your gaze and seek the skies,
For love transcends and never dies.
A glimpse of hope in darkest days,
His endless love, forever stays.

With open arms, embrace the light,
For in His love, we find our sight.
Through every moment, joy will reign,
A glimpse of peace through every pain.

When Angels Whisper Absent

In shadows deep, where silence dwells,
The heart it listens, and softly swells.
When angels whisper, though unseen,
Their presence felt, a love serene.

Through trials faced, and tears we shed,
In every sorrow, hope is fed.
A guiding hand, though far away,
In whispered truths, they gently stay.

We find our strength in weary days,
As light prevails in shadowed ways.
In every prayer, our spirits soar,
When angels whisper, we endure.

Their voices echo in the night,
A sacred song, our hearts alight.
With every breeze, their love we feel,
In deepest grief, their comfort heals.

Hold on to faith when dark clouds roam,
For whispers guide our steps back home.
In every absence, love remains,
When angels whisper, hope sustains.

Echoes of the Unsaid

In silent prayer, our hearts convey,
The truths that linger, night and day.
A gentle light, a guiding hand,
In whispers shared, through love we stand.

By sacred dawn, we seek the grace,
In every tear, we find our place.
The echoes of hope, though softly tread,
Fill the silence with words unsaid.

In every heart, a story breathes,
With faith entwined in autumn leaves.
Together we walk, through trials thick,
In faith's warm glow, our spirits flick.

The humble path, a narrow seam,
In whispered thoughts, we weave our dream.
Through shadows deep, a prayer we send,
Embracing the love that knows no end.

So let the echoes find their way,
In every night, and every day.
For in the silence, truths align,
In hearts united, our souls entwine.

Heavenly Parting

When twilight falls, and shadows blend,
A soft goodbye, where hearts transcend.
In gentle light, the spirit flies,
To realms of peace, beyond the skies.

With every breath, we cherish time,
In sacred bonds, our souls do climb.
The love we shared, an endless song,
In memory's arms, we still belong.

As dawn awakens, a whispered prayer,
Across the void, we feel you there.
In every star that lights the night,
Your gentle spirit, our guiding light.

Though earthly chains may hold us fast,
In faith we find, love's shadows cast.
For every tear, a flower grows,
In heavenly gardens, the truth bestows.

So let us rise, though parting's near,
In every heart, your voice we hear.
With gratitude, we hold the grace,
Of love eternal, in time and space.

The Whispered Benediction

In morning light, a prayer takes flight,
On whispered winds, it feels so right.
Each word a blessing, soft and pure,
With hope and love, our hearts endure.

As shadows linger, grace unfolds,
We share the stories, softly told.
In sacred moments, time stands still,
Our spirits dance to love's sweet thrill.

With gentle faith, the heart extends,
To all we meet, our love transcends.
In every smile, a light bestowed,
A whisper's strength across the road.

Through trials dark, we find the way,
In every night, we mold the day.
The whispered benediction flows,
In quiet hearts, where love still grows.

So let us carry this sacred thread,
In every word, where hope is fed.
For in our lives, as one we blend,
The whispered love, that has no end.

Veils of Unspoken Farewell

Beneath the stars, a silence drapes,
In shadows deep, our spirit shapes.
With every sigh, a story fades,
In veils of twilight, love invades.

Each step we take, a memory sighs,
In whispered words, where true love lies.
Through gentle nights, we seek the dawn,
In every heart, a hope reborn.

Through veils unseen, our souls unite,
In sacred bonds, the heart takes flight.
With every tear, a blessing flows,
In quiet grace, the love still grows.

So let us walk on paths unknown,
In every heartbeat, love is shown.
For in the silence, truths reveal,
The veils of farewell, time cannot steal.

As life unfolds, we kiss the pain,
In memories sweet, we'll meet again.
For love's embrace will see us through,
In veils of grace, I'll wait for you.

The Sacred Exchange of Farewell

In the hush of dusk, souls entwine,
Words hang heavy, yet hearts align.
Through tears like rain, a blessed trance,
We part in grace, a sacred dance.

Each embrace holds a whispered prayer,
An echo of love, a promise rare.
With gentle hands, we set apart,
A holy bond, woven in heart.

The paths we tread may drift and sway,
Yet light will guide us on our way.
In memories bright, we find our peace,
In every parting, love's increase.

As twilight descends, we bow our heads,
In reverence for the life that spreads.
With faith, we walk the road unknown,
In every season, we are not alone.

Farewell is but a moment's grace,
In time's embrace, we find our place.
A sacred exchange in love's pure light,
Our spirits soar, taking flight.

Kneeling in the Quietude

In stillness found, the heart takes pause,
Kneeling low, in reverence and cause.
The whispers of grace fill the night air,
A moment sacred, a tender prayer.

Soft shadows dance in the fading light,
Illuminating truth, dispelling fright.
In quietude, the spirit unfolds,
A whisper of wisdom, gentle and bold.

With hands outstretched, the soul seeks more,
Yearning for peace, to be restored.
Each breath a promise, each sigh a plea,
In the silence, I find Thee.

The world fades away, its clamor dies,
I rise on wings, closer to the skies.
In this hallowed space, I am reborn,
Kneeling in thought, for hope is sworn.

With eyes closed tight, I hear the call,
In grateful surrender, I give my all.
Kneeling down, I rise above,
In sacred silence, I feel Thy love.

The Prayerful Accords of Letting Go

In the dim light of fading day,
A heart lays bare, learning to pray.
Letting go holds a bittersweet grace,
In surrendering all, I find my place.

The mountains of burden, heavy to bear,
With faith in the journey, I grow aware.
Each tear a token, each sigh a song,
In the accords of prayer, we all belong.

Embracing the loss like a warm embrace,
In the depths of silence, I seek Your face.
The echoes of love, though shadows be cast,
In letting go, I embrace the vast.

With every heartbeat, there lies a choice,
To rise in spirit, to find my voice.
Through prayerful accords, my spirit flies,
In the act of release, my soul complies.

In this sacred dance of trust and hope,
I find my way, learn to cope.
For in letting go, I truly see,
The love that binds, forever free.

A Pilgrim's Breath at Twilight

As twilight weaves its soft embrace,
I walk the path, a sacred place.
With each step forward, I breathe in peace,
A pilgrim's heart learns sweet release.

The sky paints hues of gold and scarlet,
A canvas of dreams, so gently met.
In every sigh, moments of grace,
I find the light in this quiet space.

The journey unfolds with each heartbeat,
In humble trust, my spirit greets.
With whispered hopes and anchor deep,
A promise kept, my soul to keep.

In the stillness, I feel Your hand,
Guiding my steps on this promised land.
A pilgrim's breath, exhaling strife,
In twilight's glow, I embrace life.

The horizon beckons, new dawn awaits,
With faith as my shield, I conquer fates.
A pilgrimage blessed, I do not roam,
In every breath, I find my home.

Blessings of the Unseen

In the quiet dawn, grace descends,
Whispers of hope, the heart extends.
Invisible hands lift weary souls,
In unseen love, the spirit rolls.

Each star above, a promise bright,
Guiding our paths with gentle light.
In shadows, blessings softly gleam,
A divine embrace, our silent dream.

Through trials faced, the spirit grows,
In hidden ways, mercy flows.
Every tear, a pearl of worth,
In unseen grace, we find our birth.

Reverent Remembrance

In stillness, we gather, hearts entwined,
Reflecting on gifts that love combined.
Echoes of prayers, soft and clear,
A tapestry woven, year by year.

Each memory cherished, light in the dark,
Flickers of faith, a sacred spark.
Through trials and triumphs, we've come to know,
The depth of our bonds in gentle flow.

In moments of silence, we honor the past,
In reverent remembrance, our spirits cast.
With gratitude blooming, our hearts align,
In the embrace of love, eternally divine.

Spirit's Soft Exit

When twilight whispers, the spirit sighs,
Drifting like clouds in endless skies.
With gentle grace, the journey starts,
A final breath, as light departs.

In shadows cast, the soul takes flight,
Guided by stars, embraced by night.
A soft farewell, yet not goodbye,
For love endures, it cannot die.

With every heartbeat, memories stay,
In the silent echo of yesterday.
The spirit wanders, yet never far,
In every heartbeat, a guiding star.

The Hushed Departure

In tranquil moments, silence reigns,
A hush descends, as love maintains.
In the fading light, a spirit glows,
Wrapped in peace, as nature knows.

The world holds breath, time stands still,
Emotions stir, yet hearts are filled.
With softest grace, they slip away,
In delicate whispers of yesterday.

What once was here, now fades from sight,
Yet lives in souls, a guiding light.
In the hush, we find our way,
Through love's embrace, we gently stay.

Celestial Farewells in Twilight

As twilight falls, the stars align,
A whispered prayer, a sacred sign,
With every sunset, love draws near,
In celestial dance, we lose our fear.

Beneath the arch of heaven's grace,
We catch a glimpse of a holy place,
Each star a promise, shining bright,
Guiding our souls through endless night.

With every breath, we breathe in light,
In shadows deep, we find our sight,
The sky unfolds with tales untold,
Of love that's pure, of hearts so bold.

In prayerful moments, we embrace,
The quiet stillness, the sacred space,
A farewell spoken, never lost,
For in our hearts, love pays the cost.

So let us linger, let us weave,
The threads of faith, in dreams believe,
For every dusk gives way to dawn,
And in our hearts, love lingers on.

A Final Reverie in Prayer

In quiet moments, shadows play,
We lift our hearts, begin to pray,
A final reverie takes its flight,
In whispers soft, we find the light.

Each thought a blossom, tender, sweet,
A garden of souls where prayers meet,
In every sigh, a hope reborn,
In every loss, new strength is worn.

As dawn approaches, shadows fade,
In light's embrace, fears are outweighed,
We gather close, in unity,
Finding grace in each other's plea.

With humble hearts, we seek the way,
Through paths unknown, we choose to stay,
For in the silence, wisdom flows,
A final prayer, our spirit grows.

So let us cherish moments shared,
With love's embrace, we are prepared,
In every heart, a beacon glows,
A final reverie, love bestows.

The Soul's Gentle Exit

In twilight's embrace, the spirit drifts,
To realms unseen, where silence gifts.
With whispered prayers, the heart does mend,
A journey begun, where shadows blend.

Softly it flows, like a river's song,
A path of light, where the soul belongs.
In the hush of night, it finds its rest,
Embraced by love, forever blessed.

As the world fades, a gentle sigh,
A tender goodbye, beneath the sky.
With each heartbeat, the memories weave,
A tapestry rich, as we grieve.

The stars awaken, their watchful gaze,
Guiding the heart through the darkest haze.
In the warmth of grace, the spirit flies,
To meet the dawn in celestial skies.

In the quiet, peace envelops the soul,
Transcending the pain, making it whole.
For in this exit, a new life begins,
A dance with the light, where love always wins.

Echoes of the Divine

In every whisper, a secret calls,
The breath of angels in sacred halls.
From shadows deep, light starts to chase,
Echoes of love, a warm embrace.

In the heart's chamber, melodies rise,
Lifting our spirits to the skies.
Each note a promise from realms above,
A symphony woven with threads of love.

Through trials endured and tears we shed,
Faith lights the path where the weary tread.
In the stillness, the divine is near,
A guiding hand wipes away each tear.

As dawn awakens with fragrant light,
Hope blooms anew, dispelling the night.
Echoes resound in a radiant choir,
Igniting the soul with heavenly fire.

In every moment, the sacred we find,
Binding our hearts in ties that bind.
With every breath, let gratitude bloom,
As echoes of the divine chase away gloom.

Unheard Farewells

In the stillness, a moment hides,
Where love lingers, though the body divides.
Silent glances and hands that touch,
Unheard farewells mean so much.

The heart remembers each whispered word,
As the spirit takes flight, undeterred.
In shadows cast by the fading light,
A promise awaits in the coming night.

Though parting feels heavy, the bond remains,
In memories cherished, love never wanes.
The journey continues beyond our sight,
In the dance of stars, in the embrace of night.

Each breath taken holds echoes of grace,
A connection alive in time and space.
In the softest sigh, the soul will find,
That goodbye gives way to the divine.

And as the dawn brings forth new days,
The heart finds peace in immeasurable ways.
Unheard farewells are but bridges we cross,
Uniting our spirits, never a loss.

The Stillness of Spirit

In the hush of dawn, the spirit awakes,
A tranquil journey, where silence takes.
Through still waters, a deepening grace,
In the heart's haven, there's a sacred space.

The world spins on, yet here I stand,
Wrapped in the warmth of the Creator's hand.
With every breath, the essence flows,
In the stillness, the spirit knows.

As nature whispers, the trees align,
Reminding us all of the grand design.
In the gentle sway, the truth unfolds,
Revealing the beauty that love upholds.

In quiet moments, the soul does soar,
Finding strength in the peace we adore.
Within the stillness, wisdom resides,
Leading us forth, where love abides.

As night prevails, stars brightly gleam,
In the stillness of spirit, we dare to dream.
For life's great journey is ever profound,
In the stillness of spirit, love knows no bounds.

Laments Beneath the Stars

In the quiet night we weep,
Beneath the heavens' vast expanse.
Whispers of lost hopes we keep,
In reverence, our hearts dance.

Stars like tears, they brightly shine,
Guiding us through our darkest fears.
Each twinkle tells a tale divine,
Of love that wipes away our tears.

Oh, the moon, she listens close,
To every prayer we softly send.
In her glow, we find our dose,
Of peace that lingers without end.

Yet shadows creep, our burdens weigh,
As we search for solace there.
In silence, we long for the day,
When hope replaces every care.

Still, the stars persist to gleam,
In the sorrow of nights so long.
In their light, we dare to dream,
Together, we rise, proud and strong.

The Presence of Absence

In the echoes of empty halls,
A presence lingers on the air.
Whispered prayers break down the walls,
As we search for what was there.

Hearts that ache with quiet loss,
Find solace in the silent night.
Memories become a cross,
We bear with love, with all our might.

Yet in absence, shadows play,
Teach us lessons in their wake.
Love transcends both night and day,
In every yearning, hearts awake.

Moments shared are never gone,
They intertwine with grace and light.
In the bond that lingers on,
We find the courage to ignite.

So we cherish what remains,
In the stillness, hope appears.
Through the joy and through the pains,
We embrace the sacred spheres.

Threads of Faith Woven Softly

In the loom of life we weave,
Threads of faith in colors bright.
Stitch by stitch, we do believe,
In the tapestry of His light.

Each moment sewn with prayerful care,
Every joy and sorrow shared.
Stronger now, the bonds we bear,
In unity, our hearts are bared.

Through trials' loom, the yarn can fray,
Yet beauty flows through every tear.
Hope rekindles a brighter day,
As love binds us ever near.

Woven softly, our spirits soar,
A design only He can see.
In each thread, we find much more,
A perfect plan that sets us free.

So let us cherish each new thread,
In this sacred craft of grace.
With each moment tenderly spread,
We find His love in our embrace.

Release into the Divine Embrace

In the stillness, I release,
All my burdens to the sky.
Wrapped in love, I find my peace,
Trusting in the by-and-by.

Like the waves that kiss the shore,
I surrender, let go of fear.
In His arms, my spirit soars,
A refuge ever near.

Every sorrow, every sigh,
Flowing freely like a stream.
In His presence, I can fly,
Awakened from my restless dream.

Grace descends, a gentle rain,
Washing over every trial.
In this love, I feel no pain,
Only joy, and endless smile.

So I dive into the vast,
Into the divine's warm embrace.
In this moment, I am cast,
In the light of boundless grace.

The Unseen Path of the Departed

In shadows where the silence dwells,
The journey of souls begins to tell.
A whisper soft as evening's shade,
Guides those in faith, unafraid.

With gentle hands and open skies,
They walk through realms where spirit flies.
A light that shines beyond the night,
Transcending fear, embracing light.

The waves of time may ebb and flow,
Yet love remains, a constant glow.
In every prayer, their presence stays,
A bond unbroken, through all days.

The stars above, their watchful eyes,
Reflect the grace of goodbyes.
In memories sweet, they linger near,
A sacred warmth that conquers fear.

Through veils of mist, they softly tread,
While hearts remember what's unsaid.
The unseen path, a sacred thread,
With hope and faith where angels led.

Echoes of Everlasting Peace

When twilight falls, the spirits sing,
In harmony, a sacred ring.
The echoes call from realms above,
A gentle nudge, a sign of love.

In stillness deep, we hear their voice,
Through trials faced, we make the choice.
To seek the calm in tempest's roar,
And find the peace we longed for more.

In every heart, a sacred space,
Where memories bloom with endless grace.
Their laughter dances on the breeze,
A sweet reminder, blessed release.

Through every tear we shed with care,
There lies a strength we all can share.
The threads of love connect us tight,
As shadows turn to morn's soft light.

The promise holds, a whispered truth,
That life renews, preserving youth.
As echoes fade, we find our way,
To endless dawn and brighter day.

The Heart's Last Offering

In silence deep, a heart lays bare,
With gentle grace, an answered prayer.
A final gift, the soul bestows,
In every breath, true love still flows.

The burdens shed like autumn leaves,
In the light of faith, the spirit weaves.
With every heartbeat, peace descends,
A cherished bond that never ends.

In the garden of remembrance bright,
The heart's last offering takes flight.
A legacy, pure and divine,
In love's embrace, our souls entwine.

The steps we took, both near and far,
Are etched in time, like shining stars.
Together still, though miles apart,
Their rhythm lives within our heart.

The gentle touch of memories warm,
In every storm, they keep us calm.
The heart's last gift, forever true,
A compass guiding me to you.

Embracing the Unfathomable

In depths of faith, we seek to find,
The answers whispered in the mind.
To grasp the threads of mystery,
And weave them into history.

The unfathomable beckons near,
With every sigh, we shed our fear.
To walk the path, though dark it seem,
Is to awaken from the dream.

The silence speaks in sacred tones,
A language graced by ancient bones.
In every shadow, light will break,
A dance of souls, the world awake.

Through trials faced, we lean on grace,
With open hearts, we find our place.
With courage bold, the spirit soars,
In love's embrace, we fear no more.

In trusting all that lies ahead,
We gather strength from those who led.
Embracing depths we cannot see,
Awash in love's infinity.

Graceful Departures in Prayer

In tranquility's embrace, we find,
A moment to reflect, to unwind.
Hearts uplifted, spirits soar,
In prayerful whispers, we implore.

With every breath, we release the pain,
Offering love, as sweet as rain.
A gentle farewell, a soft refrain,
United in hope, we shall remain.

Through shadows of doubt, we seek the light,
Guided by faith, in the silent night.
In grace, we depart, with gratitude strong,
To the realms above, where we all belong.

Embraced by angels, we take our flight,
Finding solace, in holy sight.
Each tear shed, a prayer to ascend,
In love everlasting, we find our blend.

For every goodbye, a promise unfolds,
In sacred moments, our story is told.
With hearts intertwined, we take the leap,
In His arms we rest, forever deep.

The Soft Fade of the Beloved

The twilight whispers, a gentle embrace,
As we bid farewell, in sacred space.
Time slows down, as shadows blend,
In the soft fade, where memories mend.

The golden light, a kiss from above,
Wraps us in warmth, like endless love.
The beloved departs, yet stays in our heart,
In every moment, we're never apart.

With every tear, a cherished view,
Moments shared, forever anew.
In silent devotion, we bow our heads,
For the love that lived, and never spreads.

Each whisper of grace, a promise we keep,
In the soft fade, where souls peacefully sleep.
A radiant beacon, their spirit ignites,
Guiding us onward, through dark of night.

Through the veil of sorrow, we find our way,
In love's gentle hold, come what may.
With hands clasped tight, a prayer we share,
In the soft fade, they're always there.

A Pilgrimage to the Unknown

With each step forward, faith takes flight,
A journey unfolds, into the night.
The road less traveled, where shadows reside,
We carry our prayers, as our guide.

Through valleys of doubt, we walk with grace,
In the pilgrimage deep, we find our place.
Seeking the wisdom, of the unseen road,
With hope as our lantern, we lighten the load.

In the whispers of wind, the answers call,
In the silence of night, we stand tall.
With every heartbeat, our spirits align,
In the unknown paths, His love will shine.

The stars guide us forth, with shimmering glow,
Across the horizon, our faith will grow.
Together we wander, hand in hand,
In the heart of the journey, we make our stand.

Each mile a blessing, each pause a prayer,
In the pilgrimage sacred, we learn to care.
Embracing the journey, with smiles and tears,
In the pilgrimage of faith, we conquer fears.

Celestial Whispers of Release

In the dawn's soft light, whispers are heard,
Beneath the wings of grace, we find our word.
Celestial breezes, sweep through the skies,
In whispers of love, our spirit flies.

With every sigh, we release the chains,
In the holy silence, He knows our pains.
Guided by angels, we learn to trust,
In celestial realms, our hearts are just.

A tender release, in the still of night,
Where shadows dissipate, giving way to light.
Through trials and storms, our faith restored,
In celestial whispers, our souls are poured.

With open arms, we embrace the divine,
In moments of silence, our hearts entwine.
As stars twinkle softly, a sacred embrace,
In the whispers of heaven, we find our place.

Through realms of transition, we carry the flame,
In the celestial dance, we call His name.
A beautiful journey, we walk in peace,
In the whispers of release, our spirit finds ease.

The Still Waters Await

In tranquil depths, the spirit finds,
A place of peace, where love unwinds.
The gentle flow of grace surrounds,
In stillness deep, the heart rebounds.

Beneath the sky, the stars ignite,
A promise held, a guiding light.
The waters whisper, calm and clear,
Embracing all who wander near.

In every ripple, hope anew,
A sacred song, forever true.
The stillness calls, and souls can rest,
Within the heart's eternal quest.

As twilight falls, the shadows blend,
A journey's start, a journey's end.
With open arms, the waters greet,
Each spirit lost, in love complete.

Thus, let the river softly flow,
To guide the souls where they must go.
In stillness, faith will always stay,
The still waters, a sweet ballet.

A Sacred Passage Home

Through winding paths, the spirit roams,
In search of light, a place called home.
With every step, the heart feels blessed,
A sacred journey, in love's embrace.

The gentle breeze, it calls my name,
A whisper soft, to guide the flame.
Each star above, a beacon bright,
A promise held in the darkest night.

With memories wrapped in tender grace,
I find my peace in this holy space.
The echoes of prayers, a timeless song,
In sacred whispers, where I belong.

As footsteps lead to gates of light,
The heart ignites with pure delight.
A passage paved with love and care,
And faith unfolds, like evening air.

Within the warmth of what is true,
I find my way, I'm welcomed through.
In sacred arms, I softly roam,
With every heartbeat, I am home.

Final Blessings in the Breeze

Upon the hill, where silence dwells,
The final breath, as spirits swell.
In nature's arms, a soft release,
The wind carries whispers of peace.

Each leaf that falls, a story told,
Of love and light, of hearts of gold.
The breeze embraces, tender and near,
A final blessing, for all who hear.

In every gust, a prayer bestowed,
A journey's end, a sacred road.
With every sigh, the soul takes flight,
In gentle winds, we seek the light.

As dusk unfolds, the stars appear,
Each twinkle bright, a promise clear.
In nature's glow, the spirit flows,
A final blessing, as love bestows.

With open hearts, we stand as one,
In unity, the work is done.
With every breath, and every breeze,
Final blessings bring us to our knees.

Quietude at the Gates of Eternity

At the gates where stillness reigns,
The heart transcends all earthly pains.
In quietude, we find our way,
To realms where night meets dawning day.

The silence sings, in radiant hues,
A tapestry of holy views.
With gentle hands, the angels guide,
Inviting all who seek inside.

In sacred halls of whispered dreams,
The love of all, a river streams.
As shadows dance in soft embrace,
We merge with light, in timeless grace.

With every step, the soul takes flight,
In this vast realm, pure love ignites.
For in the stillness, truth will bloom,
At gates of peace, beyond the gloom.

In quietude, the journey ends,
A sacred bond, with love transcends.
Eternity awaits us here,
At gates of light, where all is clear.

The Peace Beyond Parting

In stillness blessed, we breathe anew,
Each moment gifted, a love so true.
The bonds unbroken, though paths may part,
In sacred whispers, we share one heart.

As twilight falls on our earthly days,
We find our solace in quiet ways.
The stars above, like angels they gleam,
Guiding our souls in a timeless dream.

For every tear, a joy remains,
In light's embrace, we cast off chains.
No fear in leaving, for we're not lost,
In peace we gather, no matter the cost.

Together we rise, through shadow and light,
Embracing love's promise that holds us tight.
In every heartbeat, our spirits sing,
The peace beyond parting, eternal spring.

So let us walk with faith in our stride,
For death is but a gentle guide.
In every ending, a new beginning,
With open hearts, we see year's spinning.

Serene Departure into Light

When dawn awakens with golden grace,
We find the warmth of a familiar face.
In gentle waves of a calming tide,
We journey forth, with love as our guide.

The path ahead may twist and turn,
Yet in our hearts, the fire will burn.
A sacred bond, held firm and tight,
In the serene departure into light.

With every breath, a prayer we weave,
In moments fleeting, we choose to believe.
That love transcends, beyond time and space,
Where souls find solace, in Heaven's embrace.

We walk in beauty, with heads held high,
Carrying dreams that will never die.
In whispers soft, and laughter divine,
In every heartbeat, our fates entwine.

As stars will light the vast, dark sea,
So shall our spirits, forever be free.
In unity's glow, no darkness remains,
In the journey's end, our love sustains.

Shrouded in Reverence

In sacred stillness, we bow our heads,
Among the echoes, where silence spreads.
With humble hearts, we seek His face,
Shrouded in reverence, wrapped in grace.

The fragrance of prayer fills the air,
Beyond all longing, beyond despair.
We chant the verses of ancient lore,
In unity blessed, forevermore.

With every tear, a healing flow,
In the depths of sorrow, new seeds we sow.
Embracing the shadows that life may send,
In faith, we trust, for love transcends.

Together we stand in love and light,
Holding each other through endless night.
As stars above shine ever bright,
We rise together, our spirits in flight.

In quiet moments, His presence we feel,
A promise of hope that time cannot steal.
Forever cherished, in our hearts remain,
The ties that bind us through joy and pain.

When Silence Speaks of Eternity

In silence deep, the heart can hear,
A melody soft, so crystal clear.
Where words are few, and faith runs high,
We find the truth that will never die.

Each moment pauses, a breath anew,
In the stillness, love whispers to you.
When shadows dance in the flickering light,
The soul takes flight, embracing the night.

Through trials faced, and journeys long,
We cherish the echoes of a sacred song.
With every heartbeat, a testament flows,
When silence speaks, the spirit knows.

In the gentle hush, we feel His grace,
As time suspended, love's warm embrace.
Together we'll tread where angels dare,
In the timeless truth, we've always shared.

So let us gather in this sacred space,
With each prayer spoke, our hearts interlace.
As silence speaks of eternity's flame,
We find our peace in the Father's name.

Hallowed Memories Left Behind

In shadows cast by ancient trees,
Whispers of the past bring peace.
Every stone, a story sung,
Of faith in hearts forever young.

Upon the altar, candles glow,
Illuminating paths we know.
Silent prayers float on the air,
A tapestry of love and care.

In laughter shared, in tears we shed,
In sacred bonds, our spirits led.
A choir of angels softly hums,
As echoes of devotion come.

With every dawn, we rise anew,
In memories, our souls construe.
The love that binds will always remain,
Through hallowed halls, a lasting chain.

Though seasons change and colors fade,
The roots of faith will never jade.
In heartbeats past and moments dear,
We find the strength to persevere.

The Last Breath of Faith

As the sun dips low in the sky,
A gentle prayer begins to sigh.
With trembling hands, we grasp divine,
In faith, the light our souls entwine.

The final moments draw so near,
Yet in the heart, there is no fear.
For every breath a promise made,
In life eternal, we are laid.

The whispers of the love we've shared,
In quiet corners, we're prepared.
With trust in grace, we softly part,
For faith's embrace warms every heart.

In twilight's glow, our spirits soar,
Boundless love forevermore.
Each heartbeat sings a sacred hymn,
As life begins on mountains dim.

In the stillness, we find our way,
In whispers of the light, we stay.
The last breath serves as our release,
In the arms of love, we find peace.

Revered Echoes at Twilight

As dusk descends and shadows knit,
Old stories in our hearts will sit.
Each whispered prayer, a gentle thread,
Weaving tales of love long spread.

In twilight's embrace, memories gleam,
Fleeting moments, a sacred dream.
With reverence, our thoughts align;
In echoes, we find the divine.

The stars awaken, shimmering light,
Guiding souls through the silent night.
A symphony of hope resounds,
In every heart where faith abounds.

In sacred circles, we convene,
Past and present, a holy sheen.
Reflecting on what once transpired,
Through trials faced, our spirits inspired.

With every dusk, a promise clear,
In every shadow, faith draws near.
Through reverent echoes, we take flight,
In unity, we greet the night.

The Quiet Passage of Time

In serene moments, time flows slow,
Each tick a gift, each whisper a glow.
With every breath, the world unfolds,
In quiet grace, life gently molds.

The sun will rise, the moon will wane,
Marking days in joy and pain.
Yet through it all, our hearts will stay,
In sacred rhythms, come what may.

In stillness, we find the divine,
In every heartbeat, life entwines.
A tapestry of dreams and grace,
In quiet moments, we find our place.

As seasons change, in faith we trust,
For in the earth, we find what's just.
With open hearts and hands held tight,
We navigate the dark and light.

In every sigh, we learn to see,
The beauty in eternity.
For time, though fleeting, leaves its mark,
In silent blessings, an eternal spark.

Reverent Shadows of What Was

In sacred halls where echoes dwell,
Soft whispers tell of love's great spell.
Each shadow cast, a story stays,
Through ages past, in holy ways.

Beneath the stars, the spirits rise,
With humble hearts, they touch the skies.
In reverence, the faithful kneel,
For what was lost, their souls can feel.

The echoes of a distant prayer,
In twilight hues, they linger there.
A tapestry of grace and light,
Awakens hope in darkest night.

With every dawn, the past remains,
In woven dreams, our love sustains.
We walk the paths where shadows fall,
In every heart, a sacred call.

Through memories, the light does gleam,
In reverent shadows, we redeem.
Embrace the past, let wisdom guide,
In holy love, we shall abide.

The Unbroken Chains of Love

In every heart, a bond so strong,
Through trials faced, where we belong.
The crucible of faith we bear,
Unbroken chains, a steadfast prayer.

In sacred vows, we lay our souls,
Through stormy seas, we meet our goals.
With hands entwined, we face the night,
The flame of love, our constant light.

Bound together, fierce and free,
Through whispered truths, we learn to be.
In every tear, a lesson given,
In every hurt, a path to heaven.

Moments shared, like stars align,
In grace, our hearts forever shine.
In trials faced, we find the way,
Unbroken love, come what may.

Rising together, we feel the worth,
In every breath, a joyous birth.
The unbroken chains that draw us near,
In love's embrace, we banish fear.

The Last Dappled Sunbeam

In twilight's glow, the world does sigh,
A last dappled sunbeam bids goodbye.
As shadows lengthen, light begins to fade,
Yet hope remains, though daylight's laid.

In sacred stillness, spirits blend,
With whispered dreams, new journeys mend.
Each fading ray holds stories told,
Of love unbound, in hearts of gold.

As night descends, the stardust gleams,
In every heart, a memory beams.
The last sunbeam, a gentle kiss,
A promise held in twilight's bliss.

Within the silence, grace unfolds,
In every shadow, love consoles.
Though daylight fades, our souls ignite,
In the last dappled sunbeam's light.

Through every dusk, we rise anew,
As dawn brings forth a sky of blue.
The last sunbeam, a fleeting glance,
Awakens dreams, a timeless dance.

Unravelling the Threads of Time

With every breath, the moments weave,
In sacred space, we learn to believe.
Threads of time, a tapestry spun,
In holy patterns, all become one.

The echoes of ages softly call,
In gentle whispers, we rise and fall.
Each heartbeat sings, a story shared,
In every touch, a love declared.

Through joy and sorrow, all entwined,
In the fabric of life, our hearts aligned.
With every thread, our spirits grow,
Unraveling paths where we must go.

Through trials faced, in faith we find,
The sacred stitches that bind mankind.
In moments treasured, lost and found,
In time's embrace, our souls are crowned.

With grace we walk, a sacred rhyme,
Unraveling the threads of time.
As journeys end, new ones commence,
In love's embrace, we find our sense.

Whispers of God's Promise

In shadows deep, His voice does call,
A gentle breeze, a soothing thrall.
With every breath, His truth we seek,
In quiet moments, He will speak.

Through trials faced, His light will guide,
With open hearts, in Him we abide.
For every sorrow, He brings grace,
In love's embrace, we find our place.

The dawn will rise, hope in its glow,
With fervent faith, we learn and grow.
A bond so pure, with spirit's flame,
In whispered prayers, we praise His name.

Each step we take, He walks beside,
In every storm, our hearts confide.
A promise kept, we cling with trust,
For in His hands, our lives He must.

Forever bound to grace divine,
With hearts as one, His love will shine.
In every moment, near or far,
We find our peace, in who we are.

The Tranquil Path Home

Upon the road, where silence reigns,
A guiding light, through joy and pains.
With every step, our hearts align,
In faith, we walk, a path divine.

The trees they whisper, secrets old,
In leaves of green, His love unfolds.
With open eyes, we see the way,
In nature's grace, we find our stay.

The river flows, like mercy sweet,
With gentle touch, it cleanses feet.
In water's song, a peace profound,
In every drop, His love is found.

As stars emerge, the night will hold,
Each spark a tale, of faith retold.
With every breath, we rise and breathe,
In harmony, our souls believe.

To journey on, with love our guide,
In every heart, He will abide.
The tranquil path, a sacred space,
In holy presence, we find grace.

Celestial Emptiness

In silent void, the stars do sigh,
A longing deep, for reason why.
With empty hands, we reach for light,
In night's embrace, we find our sight.

Each breath we take, a fragile vow,
To seek the truth, beneath the bow.
In cosmic dance, we twirl and spin,
In stillness found, the chase begins.

The void may echo, but we believe,
In faith's embrace, our hearts receive.
With every pulse, a promise bright,
In darkness, too, there shines a light.

The whispers call, from realms above,
In emptiness, we find His love.
To journey wide, through endless skies,
In cosmic threads, our spirits rise.

So let us soar, on wings of prayer,
To reach for peace, beyond despair.
In stillness deep, we learn to trust,
In divine arms, our hopes adjust.

Eternal Hues of Goodbye

The twilight falls, a soft farewell,
In fading light, our hearts do swell.
With every dusk, a memory glows,
In parting words, our true love shows.

The colors blend, in skies so vast,
As moments fade, yet memories last.
With gentle hands, we weave the threads,
In every heart, where love still spreads.

Though paths may part, our souls remain,
In sweet refrain, through joy and pain.
Each tear a jewel, each laugh a song,
In sacred ties, we still belong.

In nightfall's grace, we send our prayer,
For every soul, in love's sweet care.
As stars ignite, and moons shall rise,
In every heart, no true goodbye lies.

So let us dance, in shades of light,
For love transcends, eternal flight.
In every breath, we meet again,
In timeless hold, our souls remain.

Milton Keynes UK
Ingram Content Group UK Ltd.
UKHW021240191124
451300UK00007B/157

9 789916 791585